President Ronald Reagan's

INITIAL ACTIONS

PROJECT

Special Introduction by Arthur B. Laffer, Ph.D.

THRESHOLD
EDITIONS

New York   London   Toronto   Sydney

Threshold Editions
A Division of Simon & Schuster, Inc.
1230 Avenue of the Americas
New York, NY 10020

Introduction copyright © 2009 by Arthur B. Laffer

This Threshold Editions trade paperback edition May 2009

THRESHOLD EDITIONS and colophon are trademarks of
Simon & Schuster, Inc.

For information about special discounts for bulk purchases,
please contact Simon & Schuster Special Sales at 1-866-506-1949
or business@simonandschuster.com.

The Simon & Schuster Speakers Bureau can bring authors to your live event.
For more information or to book an event, contact the Simon & Schuster Speakers
Bureau at 866-248-3049 or visit our website at www.simonspeakers.com.

Designed by Renata Di Biase

Manufactured in the United States of America

10   9   8   7   6   5   4   3   2   1

ISBN 978-1-4391-6590-4
ISBN 978-1-4391-6593-5 (ebook)

A SPECIAL INTRODUCTION

by Arthur B. Laffer, Ph.D.

[S]hould the economy remain in its current disarray, the administration could quickly lose control of the economic policy agenda. By summer, ignited by a weak economy, the Congress could press for a host of measures to stimulate the economy generally and to shore up particularly weak sectors such as autos, housing, thrift institutions, and small businesses. Under such circumstances, the administration could easily find itself on the defensive. . . . We would essentially be reduced to reacting to events and congressional initiatives rather than shaping the economic agenda.

FINAL REPORT OF THE INITIAL ACTIONS PROJECT FOR
PRESIDENT RONALD REAGAN, JANUARY 29, 1981

LARRY SUMMERS, DIRECTOR of the National Economic Council under President Barack Obama, should be issuing such a warning for today's top policymakers instead of succumbing to the exigencies of the crowd. The above quote actually derives from a little-known policy blueprint that President Ronald Reagan followed during his first six months in office. Put together by Richard Wirthlin and David Gergen (my Yale classmate), the Initial Actions Project (IAP) is a report worth studying to compare the styles and policies of the all-time hero of conservatives, President Reagan, a man I still refer to as "the Real President," with the newly anointed liberal hero, President Obama. The similarities between early 1981, when Reagan took office, and early 2009 are uncanny.

Before delving into the IAP, let me walk you through some economic history of the United States. I am an economist, and it's obviously in my nature to judge a society by its economy, but that really *should* be how we all judge our society. Bad economics produces all sorts of collateral problems. The first of all goals is always economics. If a nation has a strong economy, the rest will fall into place. But with a bad economy, all hell breaks loose. Bad economics is the breeding ground for all sorts of other problems society faces. Unemployment is a waste of our precious resources, causing misery and personal indignity.

As is common practice in my profession, the world of political economics is divided into four all-inclusive grand partitions: fiscal policy, monetary policy, trade policy, and incomes policy. There's substantial overlap and ambiguity when it comes to the details of which actions go in which category, but the broad boundaries should be fairly understandable.

Fiscal Policy

FISCAL POLICY ENCOMPASSES the domain of government spending and taxing, whether at the federal level or at the state and local levels. And in this arena, the conceptual framework of just how fiscal policy works has been turned upside down since the mid-twentieth century. How fiscal policy actually works is discussed later.

Monetary Policy

MONETARY POLICY IS more narrowly focused on Federal Reserve policies regarding money supply, prices, and those sorts of arcana. It is unquestionably an incredibly important part of the equation. Yet because it is, at least in theory, supposed to be beyond the realm of the administration (the president nominates Fed governors, but the Federal Reserve Board is an independent body), I am going to touch on it only briefly. The story of monetary policy is the story of wisdom lost, then reacquired. Using *Star Trek* vernacular, the Prime Directive of monetary policy is to stabilize prices, thereby eliminating inflation and deflation. Just how monetary policy achieves this price stability is open to debate, but suffice it to say that inflation is basically too much money chasing too few goods. Inflation is everywhere and at all times a monetary and goods phenomenon. It is as elementary as that, my dear Watson.

And with this concept of inflation in mind, it is easy to see that more goods with the same amount of money, or less money with the same amount of goods, leads to lower prices. Higher prices are the direct consequence of fewer goods and/or more money. Stable prices require a continuous balance between the quantity of goods and the quantity of money.

Trade Policy

TRADE POLICY, OF course, has to do with imports, exports, tariffs, quotas, and other impediments to the free flow of goods and services across national boundaries. Trade policies today are unequivocally freer than they have been in many centuries. Back in the sixteenth, seventeenth, eighteenth, and even nineteenth centuries, tariffs provided the lion's share of government revenues, and customs was a major government activity. Government's malignant focus on trade peaked at the end of the third decade of the twentieth century, when the United States imposed a huge set of tariffs on imported goods collectively known as the Smoot-Hawley tariff. The pattern of stock-market collapse as this tariff legislation wended its way through the U.S. House and Senate demonstrates beyond reasonable doubt the prescience of markets.[1] What followed this massive intervention against free trade was the biggest stock-market crash in history, a period of unimaginable economic contraction and ubiquitous misery called the Great Depression.

Incomes Policy

INCOMES POLICY IS generally a catchall category for anything missed in the first three categories and includes all sorts of government actions that indirectly affect the economy, such as regulations, restrictions, and requirements such as the minimum wage, wage and price controls, Obama's health-care policy, union sanctions, and so on. Today, incomes policies may not be at their all-time lowest levels, but they are extremely close to those lows. For perspective, one has only to think back to the economic restrictions under President Dwight Eisenhower and President Lyndon Johnson or remember President Richard Nixon's and President Gerald Ford's wage and price controls or President Jimmy Carter's gasoline rationing. It was all pretty shocking.

As is only natural, the reason we concern ourselves with

---

1. For discussion of this topic and many others, I highly recommend Jude Wanniski, *The Way the World Works,* Regnery Publishing; Washington, D.C., 1998.

public economic policy is that we believe these policies matter a great deal to the health and welfare of our nation. And they do!

Now, let me walk you through the history of these economic policies in the United States and the economic results that accompanied them.

BRIEF MACROECONOMIC HISTORY
OF THE UNITED STATES

A REVOLUTION IN economic reasoning associated with the name John Maynard Keynes began in the 1930s. Keynesian economics, as it is called, was totally preoccupied with demand—or, more precisely, insufficient demand. Government policies were developed to "stimulate" demand, policies such as increasing government spending and reducing taxes (these first two items are referred to collectively as deficit spending), printing money, and devaluing a country's currency. The experience most closely associated with the ascendancy of Keynesian economics was the depression of the 1930s, following as it did on the heels of the boom of the "roaring" 1920s. In order to stabilize the cyclical movements of an economy, automatic increases in spending were tied to unemployment and low incomes. Taxes, which in the Keynesian framework dampened economic excesses, were tied to incomes in a progressive fashion so that taxes would decline disproportionately in times of recession, thereby stimulating a recovery, and rise disproportionately in times of economic excess. Likewise, easy money and currency depreciation were seen as appropriate tools to combat economic declines.

Increasingly, Keynesian thought came to dominate public policy up to and including the Carter presidency (1977–1981). By the time of the U.S. entrance into World War II, the period immediately following the Great Depression, the highest federal marginal personal income-tax rate had risen to 81 percent (after being made constitutional by the Sixteenth Amendment in 1913), and by the end of the war, that rate had risen to an unfathomable 94 percent.

From the perspective of today's America, it's hard to imagine just what the debate back then was like between liberals and conservatives. How high would tax rates have had to go before a majority in Congress felt it was gouging? Did politicians back then really believe an 81-percent tax rate was a "giveaway to the rich"? If it weren't so serious, it would have been funny.

Surprisingly, the first counterrevolution to ever-increasing tax rates occurred on President Harry Truman's (1945–1953) watch. The Revenue Act of 1945 was signed into law and repealed the excess profits tax, cut the top personal income-tax rate from 94 percent to 86.45 percent, and cut the corporate income-tax rate from 40 percent to

38 percent. It may seem at first blush like a small cut, but if you were in that top tax bracket, the cut from 94 percent to 86.45 percent actually represented a 127-percent increase in the after-tax return for each dollar of gross income on the margin (from 6 cents to 13.6 cents). Unfortunately, the relief was short-lived, and the top personal and corporate income-tax rates were raised beginning in 1950 and reached 92 percent and 52 percent, respectively, by 1952.

World War II was also a period of highly restrictive trade policies by which enemy combatants were literally embargoed; that is, all trade stopped. Following World War II, there were many policies aimed at rebuilding the world's economies, including massive foreign aid and freer trade, but trade was still far from free. In fact, it wasn't until 1958 that the continental European economies actually had convertible currencies. Before convertibility, each government had to grant special permission if one of its citizens wished to buy foreign currencies. Such policies are inconceivable today.

It wasn't until the election of President John F. Kennedy (1961–1963) that Keynesian economics received its first strong challenge in the United States. Kennedy promised huge tax-rate cuts in 1963, and he certainly delivered. The Kennedy tax cuts passed Congress and went into law in 1964, just months after he was assassinated. Kennedy cut the highest federal marginal income-tax rate from 91 percent to 70 percent and the lowest rate from 20 percent to

14 percent. He also cut the highest corporate income-tax rate from 52 percent to 48 percent. He had proposed cutting the highest corporate rate to 46 percent, but—thank goodness—the Republicans, led by Senator Barry Goldwater, were able to prevent Kennedy from doing something so rash.

Kennedy also pushed for dramatically lower tariffs on traded products with the Trade Expansion Act of 1962 and with the Kennedy Round tariff negotiations (1964–1967). His policies on trade were not universally pro–free trade, but they were a move in the right direction.

Kennedy also reaffirmed the dollar's convertibility into gold in May 1962 after jousting with French president Charles de Gaulle. Kennedy enacted the 7-percent investment-tax credit and shortened the depreciable lives for plant and equipment expenditures, all in the name of the incentives to save and invest. The Kennedy period was called the "Go-Go Sixties." The economy and the stock market had rarely been better.

Unfortunately, Kennedy's assassination ushered in the presidencies of Johnson (1963–1969), Nixon (1969–1974), Ford (1974–1977), and Carter (1977–1981)—what I (somewhat) jokingly refer to as the largest assemblage of bipartisan ignorance in our nation's history. While all of these presidents were nice people who meant well for the country, their economic policies were awful. And I say this even though I worked under Nixon and Ford.

Johnson partially reversed the Kennedy tax cuts, and his three successors continued the move away from the policies of Kennedy. Government spending went crazy, tax surcharges were routine, and the highest federal marginal tax rate on capital gains was nearly doubled.[2]

And it wasn't just their fiscal policy that was so painful. Johnson and Ford were checkered on trade policy, while Nixon, with his dollar devaluation and 10-percent import surcharge, and Carter, with his national energy plan, were outright protectionists. Meanwhile, this period almost single-handedly created the fourth grand kingdom of macro-economics (incomes policy) with all of the sparkle-headed ideas floating around Washington.

Do you remember the 1970s devaluation of the dollar? Wage and price controls? Income-tax surcharges? The "Whip Inflation Now" (WIN) buttons? It was an amazing era of truly intense Keynesian thinking. The era of Johnson, Nixon, Ford, and Carter is best summarized by the stock market. In February 1966, the Dow Jones Industrial Average barely touched 1,000. In August 1982, just before Reagan's policies took effect, the inflation-adjusted Dow was at 235. That represents a 76.5-percent decline in the real value of America's capital stock in sixteen and a half years. Now, that's a bear market.

---

2. In 1978, against Carter's wishes, a bipartisan coalition passed by a veto-proof majority a legislated cut in capital-gains tax rates known as the Steiger-Hansen bill.

Over the course of the 1970s, the tide started to turn toward a new way of economic thinking. Finally, in 1978, California voters overwhelmingly chose to reduce property-tax rates and make any future tax-rate increases difficult. Proposition 13 received national and international attention, reflecting a sea change in U.S. politics. Reagan, riding on the crest of Proposition 13 and having promised tax cuts, won the 1980 election with more than 50 percent of the vote against both of his opponents, incumbent Carter and Independent candidate John Anderson.

Proposition 13 and Reagan's presidency (1981–1989) combined to turn Keynesian economics on its head. The United States moved in the blink of an eye to supply-side economics. And not only were supply-side economic policies not Keynesian economic policies, they also were more often than not the opposite of Keynesian economic policies. Supply-side economics rests on the following tenets:

- Government spending above a certain level hurts economic growth, as do "progressive" tax rates.

- Excessive printing of money and slow real growth cause inflation, which also hurts growth.

- Devaluation of one's currency leads to offsetting inflation and thus slower growth.

- Excessive regulation, such as taxes, destroys incentives and reduces output.

ONE IDEA COMMON to both Keynesians and supply-siders was the power of tax cuts to stimulate the economy, but even here, Keynesian logic was different from supply-side logic. Different also were the details of how taxes should be cut. Keynesians wanted taxes cut most on low incomes, because the marginal propensity to spend was highest among those with the lowest incomes. We supply-side economists sought cuts in marginal tax rates, especially the highest tax rates, to increase the incentives to produce.

From the perspective of supply-side economics, government should reduce spending and cut tax rates, exchange rates should be stabilized, and money growth should be tied to a price rule. In addition, regulations and general government interference in private markets should be reduced; that is, incomes policies should be reduced to a minimum. Beginning with the Reagan revolution, the world moved back to a pre-Keynesian era of laissez-faire.

The 1980s were an era of unprecedented tax-rate cuts of virtually every variety. Reagan cut marginal tax rates on personal income, dividends, and capital gains. The Real President also saw to it that the income-tax brackets were indexed for inflation beginning in 1985.

In terms of monetary policy, Paul Volcker, who was appointed chairman of the Federal Reserve under Carter and reappointed by Reagan, became famous for his firm stand against rampant inflation.

Reagan was also exceptionally pro–free trade, successfully backing several major rounds of tariff reductions (although he did from time to time impose one-off protectionist measures). Finally, Reagan decontrolled oil and waged a war against excessive regulation. One of the most memorable events of my lifetime was when Reagan fired the striking air-traffic controllers. Also, the television image of Reagan dropping the Federal Register of government regulations said it all. Under Reagan, the federal minimum wage was never increased.

Reagan's results were amazing. The economy and the stock market soared. Interest rates and inflation collapsed. Strikes and race riots virtually vanished, and America was back as the protector of world peace.

While there was a little slide back on fiscal policy and incomes policy under President George H. W. Bush, President Bill Clinton continued Reagan's supply-side legacy. Although he did raise the highest marginal tax rate, he also cut government spending as a percentage of GDP by 3.5 percentage points (more than the best four presidents at cutting spending combined), enacted the largest capital-gains tax cut in our nation's history, pushed NAFTA through Congress, got rid of the retirement earnings test for Social Security, and passed welfare reform. All in all, Clinton was a good president, and the economy showed it. Stock prices, employment, and output all soared under Clinton.

The supply-side movement even gained some further momentum during George W. Bush's first term through increased free trade and reductions in the highest marginal tax rates on personal income, dividends, capital gains, and inheritance.

PRESIDENT REAGAN

RETURNING TO THE Initial Actions Project, Reagan was elected in the midst of what legitimately was the worst recession since the Great Depression. Unemployment and inflation were both running in double digits, and he was elected on the promise of a new path for America. The focus most certainly was on the economy.

The IAP was put together as the political blueprint for what we now call Reaganomics. The level of detail in the final report is absolutely astonishing. It examines the roots of Reagan's electoral victory and applies that to his ability to lead the country to his desired outcomes, both short-term and long-term, in the realms of economic policy, foreign policy, and domestic policy. The report even analyzes the first one hundred days of the terms of past presidents for insights into presidential behavior, scheduling, travel, meetings, appearances, and the like. It was only through this careful preparation that the Reagan administration was able to move the United States to supply-side economics.

Following on the design laid out in the IAP, in August 1981, Reagan signed into law the Economic Recovery Tax Act (ERTA, also known as Kemp-Roth). ERTA slashed marginal earned-income tax rates by 25 percent across the board over a three-year period. The highest marginal tax rate on unearned income dropped to 50 percent from 70 percent immediately (the Broadhead Amendment), and the tax rate on capital gains also fell immediately from 28 percent to 20 percent.

These across-the-board marginal tax-rate cuts, sound money, freer trade, and reduced regulations combined to yield higher incentives to work, produce, and invest. And the economy responded. Between 1978 and 1982, the economy grew at a 0.9-percent rate in real terms, but from 1983 to 1986, this growth rate increased to 4.8 percent.

Before Reaganomics, the economy was choking on high inflation, high interest rates, and high unemployment. All three of these economic bellwethers dropped sharply after Reagan's policies took effect.[3] The unemployment rate, which had peaked at 9.7 percent in 1982, began a steady decline, reaching 7.0 percent by 1986 and 5.3 percent when Reagan left office in 1989.

---

3. To discern the effects of Reaganomics on the economy, I use the starting date of January 1, 1983, given that the bulk of the cuts were in place on that date. However, a case could be made for a start date of January 1, 1984, the date when the full cut was in effect.

INTRODUCTION

Inflation-adjusted revenue growth dramatically improved. Over the four years before 1983, federal income-tax revenue declined at an average rate of 2.8 percent per year, and total government income-tax revenue declined at an annual rate of 2.6 percent. Between 1983 and 1986, these figures were a positive 2.7 percent and 3.5 percent, respectively.

The most controversial portion of Reagan's tax revolution was the big drop in the highest marginal income-tax rate from 70 percent when he took office to 28 percent in 1988. However, Internal Revenue Service data reveal that tax collections from the wealthy, as measured by personal income taxes paid by top-percentile earners, increased between 1980 and 1988 despite significantly lower tax rates.

PRESIDENT OBAMA

IN MANY WAYS, Obama has fashioned his transition to
the presidency after Reagan's transition. Like Reagan, he
has inherited an economy in a deep recession, and he has
made great efforts to communicate the reasons behind his
policy actions. In other ways, however, Obama's transition
is a disaster by comparison. A variety of incidents indicate
that a detailed plan such as the Initial Actions Project is
missing. From letting Senate majority leader Harry Reid
and Speaker of the House Nancy Pelosi write the stimulus
package, to the publicly scrutinized tax problems of several
potential presidential appointments, to having Commerce
Secretary nominee Senator Judd Gregg pass up the chance
to serve in the administration, citing irreconcilable differ-
ences on the economy, Obama has made a number of mis-
steps in his first fifty days.

Far more substantially, Obama is reversing the very
successful policies of Kennedy, Reagan, and Clinton.

One only needs to look as far as the stimulus bill that the president pushed through Congress. The whole theory that these people are espousing revolves around the notion that the people who receive these funds will be stimulated into working and consuming, which is true. But they never look at the people from whom those resources are taken, the people who will be destimulated. Income effects will be net to zero in an economy, and there is no stimulus in these stimulus packages.

If you give people command over real resources based on some characteristic other than work effort, those real resources can come only from workers and producers. So, every time the government makes a transfer payment, remember that there is no Tooth Fairy. Every dollar spent to bail out one group has to come from another group of people—namely, workers and producers. It drives a wedge between wages paid and wages received, and actually reduces the amount of pay going to people who produce. This equates to a movement downward on the supply curve, which reduces output, employment, and production. So, these stimulus packages not only do not stimulate, but they actually hurt the economy. And the magnitude of it all is simply astounding.

All of Obama's and the Congress's actions are having a terrible effect on the budget deficit and debt numbers. The projected federal budget deficit for 2009 went from $482 billion dollars, or 3.1 percent of GDP, when estimated in

July 2008 to the current estimate of $1.566 trillion, or 12 percent of GDP, as projected by the Office of Management and Budget. Accordingly, the federal debt will rise from a recent low of 35 percent of GDP in 2001 to upward of 75 percent or 100 percent of GDP by the end of 2009.

With the huge increases in government spending and accompanying run-up in the national debt, it's little wonder that Obama is proposing tax increases. His first budget proposed raising the highest marginal tax rate on personal income from 35 percent to 39.6 percent, raising the highest marginal tax rate on capital gains and dividends from 15 percent to 20 percent, taxing carried interest from partnerships at personal income-tax rates rather than capital-gains-tax rates, decreasing deductions available to upper-income earners, and instituting a cap-and-trade program, which is really just a fancy name for a tax on carbon without any offsetting decrease in other taxes. The cap-and-trade program alone is estimated to cost $646 billion in new taxes.

When it comes to monetary policy, Fed chairman Ben Bernanke is the anti-Volcker. The Fed has presided over the most dramatic increase in the money supply in the history of our nation. The monetary base has grown from about $860 billion in January 2008 to about $1.57 trillion today.[4] That is a doubling of the monetary base. There has

4. As of March 11, 2009, the monetary base was about $1.566 trillion, down from a high of $1.750 trillion recorded four weeks earlier.

been no thought given to taking these reserves out, even though, repeating Milton Friedman, "Inflation is everywhere and always a monetary phenomenon."

In terms of trade policy, Obama campaigned on such an anti–free trade campaign that his lead economist, Austan Goolsbee, was kept out of the spotlight for several weeks of the campaign after whispering to Canada that candidate Obama was not serious about renegotiating NAFTA. Obama has since allowed "Buy American" clauses into his stimulus bill, forced Swiss cooperation on targeting UBS investors who may have cheated on their taxes, made it harder to hire skilled immigrants through the Employ American Workers Act, refused to take up completed free-trade agreements with Colombia and South Korea, and attacked domestic companies that don't repatriate the earnings of foreign subsidiaries. All in all, his policies are downright hostile to trade and probably the most protectionist we have seen since Carter.

Finally, Obama is a disaster on incomes policies as well. He wants to institute a cap-and-trade policy that will have the effect of making energy more expensive and more volatile in price, to make us energy-independent, to institute universal health-care coverage, and to give more power to unions by getting rid of the secret ballot and mandating that government contracts pay the highest prevailing union wage.

SUMMARY

IT'S CLEAR THAT Obama is a student of history and has a great deal of respect for former president Reagan. There are even reports of Obama's aides specifically seeking out members of the Reagan administration for advice. Furthermore, during the campaign, then-Senator Obama opined that "Ronald Reagan changed the trajectory of America in a way that Richard Nixon did not and in a way that Bill Clinton did not. He put us on a fundamentally different path because the country was ready for it."[5]

Whereas Reagan and his team developed the Initial Actions Project to direct their path toward Reaganomics, the Obama administration seems lost. Even worse, when the Obama administration does present an economic policy, that policy is most frequently opposed to growth. Whether fiscal policy, monetary policy, trade policy, or incomes

---

5. Obama interview with *Reno Gazette-Journal* Editorial Board, January 14, 2008.

policy, the current policy dials are all turned in the wrong direction.

The economics of Reagan and Obama obviously are at opposite ends of the spectrum, and one could easily have reached the same conclusion by just looking at the immediate goals of each president. Reagan had the following three goals in his first few months in office:

1. The air-traffic controllers who were on strike would be fired and could never again work for the government.

2. He would remove Carter's controls on the price of oil.

3. He would do whatever it took to generate the release of the American hostages at the U.S. embassy in Iran.

FORTUNATELY, IRAN KNEW Reagan's resolve on the third point and released the hostages fifteen minutes before he walked onstage for his inaugural address, thus removing that action item. But the other two points made clear what comes through in the IAP: Reagan was a man who knew the ideal policies that lead to economic growth, and he was the man to remake America as the "shining city on the hill."

Now, compare Reagan's goals with Obama's first address to Congress, in which the three main points of focus were national health care and ever greater state intervention in education and the environment. Obama's first executive order allowed government agencies to require government contractors to unionize in order to receive government contracts. This is a president who wants to overturn the successful pro-growth legacy that Reagan started with the IAP. And believe me, if you reverse the policies of Reagan, you should expect the opposite results.

FINAL REPORT OF THE

INITIAL ACTIONS PROJECT

January 29, 1981

SECTION I

OVERVIEW

INTRODUCTION

DURING THE FIRST week of the Reagan Administration, the attention of all Americans focused primarily on the return of the hostages, arousing patriotic pride and providing a brief respite from other major concerns.

Nevertheless, a sense of urgency still surrounds the initial action agenda of the presidency of Ronald Reagan. The direction of the country remains unsatisfactory to a majority of Americans. Hoping for change, they elected Ronald Reagan to preside over a restructuring and redirecting of public policy for the country. The public sense of urgency requires that the new President immediately undertake to steer a new course, to advance policies designed to support that new direction, and to follow those policies with firmness and consistency.

The initial days of the new Reagan Administration will be the time when his presidency will be under its closest scrutiny. What is done or not done may well cast the die for what is recorded about the entire four-year performance of the first Reagan Administration. How we begin will significantly determine how we govern. Certainly the people and the pundits will start asking whether the Reagan Administration constitutes a juncture in American history when the role of the federal government was changed and a "new beginning" was commenced along the lines of Mr. Reagan's approach to governance.

The first actions of the administration must be taken in the context of the situational inheritance that is assumed from previous administrations. That context requires the focus of this early period to be on the plight of the American economy, the federal budget, and the uncertainty of America's role in world affairs.

1980 may well have been the most critical year for the American economy in half a century. The persistence of double-digit inflation has resigned many to the expectation that such rates are now a permanent part of the American economic landscape. Moreover, the pattern of government expenditures and revenues during the last half of the year illuminated more dramatically than ever before the extent to which the federal budget is out of control. <u>No American President since Franklin Roosevelt has inherited a more difficult economic situation</u>.

The prevailing sense among many Americans, and the country's allies and adversaries, is that the United States is uncertain of its national interests and role in world affairs.

U.S. foreign policy has recently been fraught with ambiguity, uncertainty, and inconsistency. Worse still is the growing view that America has grown weak in its foreign policy resolve, in its defense posture, and in its ability to respond to security threats around the globe.

Nothing destabilizes the international system more than a superpower that has lost its way in the world.

INITIAL STRATEGIC CONSIDERATION

THE BEGINNING OF any new administration has tremendous short-term costs and demands—and opportunities. In the beginning, the forces driving the momentum of presidential action are almost exclusively external to the president himself. It is, therefore, essential to develop, integrate, and heed a few strategic considerations in order to give coherence and structure to the Reagan Administration's first steps. We consider these strategies under four rubrics—The Presidency; The Political Environment; Action: Timing and Sequence; and Policy.

The Presidency

- Presidential leadership is maintained by consistency, commitment, and resolve. Too frequently, presidents declare they will be consistent and resolute without fully realizing that the proof is in the policies they adopt. A president must begin doing in the first few days what he promised during the campaign.

- To be effective in this initial three- or four-month period, President Reagan should focus his attention on the key strategic policy objectives—namely the President's economic package and the task of restoring U.S. credibility in world affairs.

- The momentum of presidential activity—a brisk but not frantic pace in the beginning—emphasizes the sense of urgency and provides the basis for the President's leadership opportunity. The times support policy changes.

- The presidency thrives when bold, imaginative leadership is exhibited, and withers when a president fails to give the country a clear sense of direction and vision.

- The image of being a warmonger, narrowly pro–big business, and uncaring could potentially derail the President's aspirations of a new direction for the country.

Political Environment

- The Congress, the bureaucracy, the press, and the public will be looking for early clues which may signal how the new administration will conduct its relations with the power centers in Washington. Early impressions persist, hence the degree of openness and frequency of consultation established early in the term will likely determine the pattern for the next four years. The President should follow up on his earlier efforts to demonstrate a desire to work with, rather than around, Washington's establishment.

- The times are conducive (if not demanding) of policy change; the public is prepared, even anticipates, that President Reagan will initiate substantial changes in federal policy.

- During the campaign an electoral coalition was successfully formed, and during the initial phase of the new administration it is essential to build a governing coalition based on the constituencies brought together in the electoral coalition and then broadened to include the constituencies necessary to govern the country. To do this successfully we must practice the art of accommodating a variety of public aspirations to public goals that are consistent with our own identified policies.

• The limits of presidential power in a representative democracy are ultimately set by the public's support for the President's policies. Consensus and coalition building are the processes by which the President expands the parameters of his influence and effectiveness.

• Expectations are the ultimate source of public frustration. There are high performance expectations associated with Mr. Reagan's presidency. Caution should be exercised not to further enhance expectations, and boldness should be observed in fulfilling the promise to revitalize the economy and enhance U.S. security.

• The public is predisposed to believe the new President can change the direction of the country, but they are yet to be convinced that Mr. Reagan's policies will work. The President's substantial communication skills are required to generate the public and congressional support necessary for their success.

Action: Timing and Sequence

- Undertake the difficult early. There is never an easy time to do arduous tasks. The window of opportunity opens and closes quickly; therefore, the President needs to take the initiative early and decisively.

- The momentum of presidential activity—a brisk but not frantic pace in the beginning—emphasizes the sense of urgency.

Policy

- The President's focus should be on the outlining of broad strategic policy outlines, and not on narrow programs.

- The President's policy credibility must be established early in the presentation and defense of difficult policies. It is essential that the President's public presentation of policy be simple, straightforward, and understandable.

- In the process of establishing a cabinet government where policy authority is delegated to the respective secretaries and directors, it is imperative to retain the idea that the President is in charge and there is a steady hand at the helm.

- It is essential that long-term policy options should not be foreclosed by narrow, short-term policy options.

- The magnitude of the economic/budget package and the fact that it is the policy centerpiece of the new administration will require that the administration expend considerable political influence to secure its passage and successful implementation. In effect, the first ninety days are critical because the administration will be expending so much of its political muscle to pass an economic revitalization package. It is important to realize that while the issue is economic, the capital expended is political.

CONCLUSION

A PERUSAL OF the above strategic considerations makes it clear that of all the demanding roles, functions, and titles a president carries, such as Commander in Chief, Leader of Party, Chief Executive Officer—the ones that will be most crucial in this initial period of Ronald Reagan's governance will be Teacher, Communicator, and Motivator. He must convey in simple, uncluttered ways a sense of direction that will provide hope for Americans who want, above all else, a strong leader to lead.

SECTION II

ROOTS

THE MAJOR OBJECTIVES and strategies to be considered in the opening stages of the Reagan Presidency should, for the sake of consistency and continuity, find their roots in the social-political-economic environment that conditioned the Ronald Reagan November landslide. That consistency will assure the strengthening of our governing base and ease the implacement of our policies as much as or more than any other single factor. Ultimately our power to govern rests with the support of a majority of the people.

An examination of those roots past, present, and future provides the best single frame of reference for the discussion that follows concerning our initial policy objectives.

We outline below those roots under the rubrics of:

- Past—The 1980 Electoral Mandate: Frame for Governing;

- Present—The Presidential Opportunity to Lead; and,

- Future—Consensus and Coalition Building, 1980–1984.

THE 1980 ELECTORAL MANDATE:
FRAME FOR GOVERNING

REAGAN'S MANDATE IS "change."

Traditionally, Americans have viewed their president as the catalyst for progress. Jimmy Carter's failed presidency, juxtaposed against Reagan's unique appeal to the hope that things can change for the better, lies at the very base of the 1980 victory. Thus, the 1980 presidential election should be viewed as an axial event demarking a major political opportunity for redrafting the policy agenda of this country.

The election was not a bestowal of political power, but a stewardship opportunity for us to reconsider and restructure the political agenda for the next two decades. The public has sanctioned the search for a new public philosophy to govern America.

In sum, Governor Reagan won because he, not Carter or Anderson, articulated an approach to governance, reflected an awareness of the role of leadership in motivating masses of individual citizens, and provided a sense of vision about America's future direction. Political leaders in America reduce uncertainty about the future not because they have ready-made solutions for all problems, but rather because they give expression to the essential tenets of an overall approach to both public policy and governance that rings a responsive chord among a broad swath of the electorate.

The central features of Reagan's basic approach that built the 1980 electoral mandate were:

- Trust the values of American society that are largely responsible for sustaining its <u>growth</u>.

- Treat America's leaders, public and private, as accountable stewards responsible for living up to those commonly shared values of family, work, neighborhood, peace, and freedom.

- Recognize the inherent value of individual initiative and the operating premise of a representative democracy that government—federal, state, and local—should not perform functions that are better handled by individual citizens on their own behalf.

- General solutions to the major problems now besetting our society by explicitly recognizing that three major conditions have darkened the visage of America. Specifically they are:

- The federal government's size and cost have exceeded what is reasonable and have led to the government often doing what is unnecessary and too frequently missing the mark on what is really needed.

- A sluggish economy and double-digit high inflation are principally caused by excessive government spending, taxation, and an over-regulated private enterprise sector.

- A once-proud and powerful America has acquiesced to a secondary role in the world.

THE SPECIFIC MANDATE calls for a recasting of those three conditions.

As we begin to form a government and create its policies against the frame of reference of our electoral mandate, we should keep in mind that political mandates generate both their form and force from expectations. Similarly, expectations also condition strongly presidential successes and failures.

After the election, Carter noted that, "One of the

anomalies of this election is that things on which I worked the hardest were the ones that were politically counterproductive." He then cited the Panama Canal, the Mid-East peace talks, and human rights policies as particularly damaging to him politically.

More to the point, however, may be the fact that four years ago when Mr. Carter arrived in Washington, he committed to a sweeping consolidation of many federal agencies into a few. Instead he ended up adding the Departments of Energy and Education to the Cabinet. He was going to save millions with "zero based-budgeting." He was going to reform a tax system that was "a disgrace to the human race." He hoped in his inaugural address that "nuclear weapons could be eliminated from the face of the earth." Hence, Jimmy Carter established in the first few months the foundation for the shearing comparisons between his promises and performances by the way he uniquely shaped and created expectations which fueled the antagonisms that helped to defeat him. What we do, say, and symbolize in the first months are critical strategically. Thus, we should keep in mind that mandates when viewed as "expressions of collective will" not only can impact who wins or loses elections, but also can shape and mold how successfully a president is able to govern.

In sum, the Reagan Administration four years hence will be judged both on the basis of what it accomplishes as well as the expectations it generates in its early months.

But ultimately our success rides on whether things by 1984 "have changed for the better," when more Americans, one hopes, will answer the question, "Are you better off now than you were four years ago?" with a resounding "Yes!"

If so, our mandate will have been met.

THE PRESIDENTIAL
OPPORTUNITY TO LEAD

WHILE AMERICANS DEMAND a great deal from a president, they are willing to entrust him with considerable authority to lead. Fully seven out of ten voters agreed with the statement, "A few good leaders could make this country better than all the laws and the talk." (Decision/Making/Information, Post-Election Study: November 1980)

More specifically, Thomas Cronin observed correctly that:

> *Only the President can be the genuine architect of the United States public policy, and only he, by attacking problems frontally and aggressively and by interpreting his power expansively, can slay the dragons of crisis and be the engine of change to move this nation forward.*
>
> *The President must be the nation's personal and moral leader; by symbolizing the past and future*

*greatness of America and radiating inspirational con-
fidence, a President can pull a nation together while
directing its people toward fulfillment of the American
Dream. (The State of the Presidency, p. 84)*

RONALD REAGAN WON the 1980 presidential election
because a majority of voting Americans ultimately came
to believe that he had the <u>leadership qualities</u> necessary to
deal more effectively with the country's major problems.
Specifically, during the course of the election the Governor created the expectations that he was the best hope to
reduce inflation and restore America to a position of pre-
dominance in the world.

The most unfulfilled expectation of the earlier Ford/
Carter encounter was that a leader had emerged who could
supplant disarray with order, mismanagement with management, and malaise with confidence. Some media com-
mentators have suggested that Americans now believe that
"After all is said and done, it really doesn't matter who is
elected President since things won't change much anyway."
This does not reflect the sentiment of our citizens today.
Almost eight out of ten (76%) reject this notion (Deci-
sion/Making/Information <u>Post-Election Study: November
1980</u>). The public yearned for a national leader in 1976,
but the disheartening evidence of the Carter term was that
he was unable to satisfy the national desire for leadership

which could restore the country to its proper bearings. In that sense, 1980 was a replay of the 1976 election: it was a referendum on national leadership focusing particularly on the economy.

This was precisely the theme of the campaign, precisely the attraction of Ronald Reagan as a candidate, and precisely the reason for the victory.

Ronald Reagan was elected because he, more than any other national candidate, projected the image of a leader with the attributes they most wanted in a President of the United States. The Decision/Making/Information Post-Election Study clearly reflects that:

- On all of the candidate attributes which are leadership related, Reagan outpolled Carter.

- Voters for whom leadership was a critical attribute influencing their vote strongly preferred Reagan to Carter.

- Specifically, when asked which of the three candidates was best described by several phrases, we learned that:

    - 61% believed Mr. Reagan had the strong leadership qualities this country needs; and,

- 71% of the voters think Ronald Reagan offers the single best hope to reduce inflation.

OTHER PRESIDENTIAL LEADERSHIP perceptions of the President-elect were reported by Lou Harris from a post-election study (1,200 adults, nationwide):

	Agree	Disagree
He (Ronald Reagan) has a highly attractive personality and will inspire confidence in the White House.	69%	27%
He is no ordinary politician because he really wants to cut federal spending and cut back the federal bureaucracy.	66	30
He really cares about working people and minorities and will help get jobs for the unemployed.	55	38

- While it is good to have   90   9
  someone who is firm with
  the Russians as President,
  he has to guard against
  getting the U.S. into
  another war.

- As President he has to be   73   25
  careful not to be too close
  to big business.

PERHAPS MORE TO the point of the leadership opportunity the November election presents, Decision/Making/Information asked the question:

"What good thing do you think will happen to you and your family now that Ronald Reagan has been elected President?"

"KEEP PRICES UNDER control" surfaced as the strongest positive expectation (27%), followed by the more general "improve the economy" (26%), then "re-establish strong leadership, better government" (20%), "improve U.S. foreign policy (15%), and "cut taxes" (15%). Seven out of ten could articulate at least one good thing they thought would happen now that Ronald Reagan is our 40th President. Contrarily, in the last days of October, less than half could identify a good thing they expected Jimmy Carter might accomplish if re-elected.

We have discussed above the unique roots of our 1980 victory by reviewing the nature of the electoral mandate and the Presidential opportunity to lead. Now we turn to the future by focusing on consensus and coalition building.

CONSENSUS AND
COALITION BUILDING

IT WOULD BE easy in the flush of victory to conclude that those who politically cast their lots for a Reagan Presidency somehow are ours to keep if only we do a credible job. Yet our 1980 support might last just a fleeting moment unless, in addition to doing a credible job, we now proceed to build coalitionally a victory that will abide.

Coalition building, for the purpose of this discussion, is the process of constructing majorities from the broad sentiments and interests of the populace that can be found to bridge the narrower needs and hopes of separate individuals in the community. If completely successful, coalition building yields consensus. To do this successfully we must practice the art of accommodating a variety of public aspirations to public goals that are consistent with our own identified policies.

Durable coalitions do not just happen, they <u>are</u> built.

Examining the particular pattern of vote behavior that generated Ronald Reagan's electoral landslide as well as helped defeat five previously unbeatable liberals in the Senate and scored gains of almost unprecedented dimensions for the Republicans in the House all provide strong evidence that the 1980 election broke the New Deal hold by shattering its historical coalition.

Against that euphoric read of the election, we should, however, keep in mind that while Ronald Reagan polled 51% of the support of those who voted, nevertheless:

- Right after the election, only 13% of the electorate indentified themselves as strong Republicans.

- Almost one-half (48%) of those eligible to vote did <u>not</u> cast ballots.

- As the electorate has become freed from the ties of partisanship it also exhibits almost unrestrained volatility in its support of both incumbents and challengers.

BUT AN ELECTORATE, unshackled of its partisanship, provides the opportunity to build on the vote pattern of 1980—if not a full party realignment in 1982 and 1984—at minimum, a greatly strengthened Republican coalition that can change the governing environment of the United States for the next three decades.

In order to accomplish this task we must consciously keep in focus the nature of the 1980 coalition and deal to our own long-term strengths to fashion a more favorable ambiance for all Republicans running for the office in the future.

In many respects the basic philosophical thrust of the Reagan campaign discussed above provided the consensual tool that cut across all demographic, economic, and geographic subgroups in our favor. However, it is coalition building and not the drive for consensus that has structured political success in this country almost from the time of its founding.

To understand which groups and what areas offer opportunity for coalition building, consider where the massive shifts in support occurred between the 1976 Carter election and the 1980 Reagan victory. Across all groups there was a twelve-point shift. However, the shift was considerably larger among seven particular constituent groups in the electorate.

These were: males, where the shift was 20 points; union members (16 points); high school graduates (16 points); post graduates (15 points); the middle aged—35 to 44—(15 points); Democrats (22 points); liberals (38 points); and the South, which in 1976 went strongly to Carter because of his successful appeal to regional pride, swung sharply back to us in 1980.

Against those shifts there are five major groups that appear to offer the best targets for us to build a strengthened coalition. Those groups are: union members, blue collar workers (especially Catholic), Hispanic, the middle aged, and the South.

Ronald Reagan's support among liberals was hyped because of their distaste for Carter. We cannot count on them in the future. Our ideological appeal must rest fundamentally on our conservatives, but we must broaden our base to include moderates to enhance our coalitional strength across the board.

By focusing on these five key groups as we begin to govern, we can change the ephemeral alteration of partisan voting patterns that occurred in partisan allegiance in 1980 into a more enduring change in 1982 and 1984. This would continue a trend, interrupted by Watergate, that goes back to 1968. Even in 1976 the signs of a weakened New Deal coalition were evident. Not only were these that classically made up the New Deal coalition declining in relative numbers as other members of the society expanded, but Carter's 1976 victory occurred only because, in addition to stitching together that New Deal coalition, he expanded it by cutting heavily into Ford's base in the outer South and small cities where because of his own roots he found special support. The likely Democratic presidential candidates of 1984 and 1988 will most likely not be able to refashion his unique appeal.

Therefore, the South, in particular, must be considered an area of critical importance for the establishment of our long-range coalition.

Effective policy solidifies a governing coalition as its disparate members view that policy favorably. In the next two sections we 1) block out the major strategic considerations that are consistent with Ronald Reagan's views and the key issues, and 2) enumerate the strategic objectives of our economic, domestic, and foreign policies.

In summary, then, to reflect our roots—past, present, and future—as discussed in this section, the overarching goal of the Reagan Administration over the next few years might be:

- To govern initially and subsequently so that the Reagan Presidency merits the enhanced respect and support of all Americans. This will not only strengthen our governing coalition but will also set in motion the long-term political changes that will sharply enhance the probability that the principles of governance that helped elect Ronald Reagan will be applied in our national and state power centers over the next two decades.

WE FEEL THIS can be most easily accomplished by dealing effectively with the twin economic demons of inflation and unemployment with policies that are not only bold and forceful but also policies that reflect a sense of equity and compassion for all Americans and by changing the image, both at home and abroad, of America from a declining and impotent power to a country renewed with vigor, direction, and strength.

SECTION III

POLICY INITIATIVES

ECONOMIC POLICY:
A NEW DIRECTION

<u>The 1980 Inheritance.</u> Future economic historians may well conclude that 1980 was the worst year for the American economy in half a century. The current economic indicators reveal a sluggish economy. They do not illuminate some of the more subtle and more worrisome changes that have taken place. The precipitous decline in economic activity in the last quarter of 1974 and the first quarter of 1975 (the <u>real</u> GNP declined by nearly 10 percent) was far more severe and visible than any statistics reported during the past year.

But in 1980, two events, more fundamentally alarming than a sharp, relatively brief recession, occurred. First, the U.S. financial community revealed for the first time in American history that they anticipate double-digit inflation over the foreseeable future. While most econometric models forecast that inflation will gradually decline over time, those who lend and borrow are now operating on a different assumption. This expectation that inflation at double-digit levels is a permanent feature of the American economic landscape constitutes a fundamental change in attitudes. In the spring of 1980 the prime interest rate hit 20 percent for the first time in this century. Twenty percent–plus rates returned in December and January as part of the Carter legacy to the new administration.

A second event in 1980 looms as equally ominous. The pattern of government expenditures and revenues illuminated more dramatically than ever before the extent to which the federal budget is out of control. Estimates for the FY 1981 budget during the last eight months of 1980 went from forecasting essentially a balanced budget to anticipating nearly a $60 billion deficit. Significantly, this swing was not the result of a rash of newly enacted spending programs or a tax cut. The dramatic shift was driven by entitlement programs and declining revenues from a lower than expected level of economic activity. "Uncontrollable" expenditures have now taken control of the budget.

No American president since Franklin Roosevelt has inherited a more difficult economic situation. Inflation continues at double-digit rates; unemployment remains persistently high; productivity, the key to real economic growth, is at historically depressed levels. The economic imperatives calling for an early comprehensive economic program are clear.

Fundamental Objectives. The expectation that high inflation rates are a permanent part of the economic landscape and that the budget is essentially out of control reflect in part a sense that the U.S. economy has no leadership or direction. It is true that the President's power to "control" the economy is limited and shared. In one sense, the pattern of economic activity is the result of decisions made each day by millions of consumers and businesses. In those areas where he does have influence, primarily spending, taxes, and regulation, the President shares his powers with the Congress and a wide assortment of departments, agencies, and commissions. And the crucial element of monetary policy is in the hands of an independent Federal Reserve System.

But despite these limits, the President, more than any other, can provide the major leadership thrust. The record of the last four years is instructive. Jimmy Carter announced seven major economic programs, on average a new one almost every six months. No consistent signals were transmitted from the White House. The administration shifted course several times without ever communicating a sense of direction or a destination. Both the policies and the articulation of those policies were characterized by vacillation, indecision, inconsistency, and confusion.

The lack of any fundamental principles to guide the formulation of policy was compounded by the lack of any effective decision making process. Economic policy never engaged the President's interest. He met infrequently and irregularly with his advisors. The White House economic policy machinery was dismantled and never replaced. Without any forum to build and maintain a consensus within the administration, different officials publicly contradicted one another, often unknowingly and unintentionally. No chief spokesman was identified or designated. No council or forum could produce an authoritative and binding decision. The public perception was that the process of making economic policy was confused and chaotic. And the President's intermittent bursts of concentrated interest in trying to cope with the problem only accentuated this image.

The first fundamental economic objective of the Reagan Presidency must be to restore a sense of stability and confidence, to demonstrate that there is a steady hand at the helm. This will require the development of realistic, coherent policies in an orderly, systematic way. And these policies must be articulated clearly and consistently. Eliminating the unpredictability, turbulence, and uncertainty of the past will do much in assuring the American people that the economy is no longer adrift. But knowing that there is a steady hand at the helm is not enough.

The second fundamental economic objective of the Reagan Presidency must be to convey a sense of hope, that there is a light at the end of the tunnel. In November, the American people overwhelmingly signalled their desire for a change. But repeated unfulfilled promises have made them skeptical and wary. Few believe that there are easy or quick solutions. They are ready to be convinced that sacrifices today will bring a better tomorrow. But they need something solid on which to base their hopes.

The third fundamental economic objective of the Reagan Presidency must be to place the U.S. economy on a path of sustained prosperity. Intermittent attempts to "fine tune" the economy have not worked in the past. Setting a steady, consistent long-term course can provide the basis for a sound economy.

The Elements of a New Direction. The elements of a new direction, of a comprehensive economic program, are simple and straightforward.

First, the accelerating growth in federal spending must be arrested. Severe expenditure control measures are needed to restore fiscal stability. This will require basic changes in the fuel that drives the federal budget—entitlement programs. The federal government in recent years has consistently lived beyond its means. The power of organized interests and highly mobilized beneficiaries has contributed to a congressional refusal to impose on itself a sense of priorities. An absence of powerful presidential leadership has compounded the problem. One symptom of our economic difficulties is a refusal to recognize the reality that the government cannot do all good things; meet every need; solve every problem; cure every ill. A fundamental change in the pattern of federal spending is an essential first step in a comprehensive economic program.

Second, the burden of federal taxation has sapped the vitality of the American economy and must be lifted. Last year, social security increases, bracket creep, and the windfall profits tax together accounted for the largest tax increase in U.S. history. The current incentives for spending are powerful, for saving and investing are minimal. Tax reduction measures to provide incentives for investment and new productive capacity are needed if we are to create more jobs and raise the rate of productivity growth.

Third, the U.S. economy must be freed from unnecessary and excessive governmental interference. The 1970's witnessed a massive flood of new regulations in almost every area of American life. The objectives of this surge in regulations were often noble, and much of it was necessary. But the disregard for carefully weighing costs and benefits soon led to excesses. And the fragmented nature of our regulatory structure meant that no one in the government was aware of or sensitive to the aggregate costs imposed on various industries or sectors of the economy. Like the growth in federal spending, this pattern must be reversed.

Addressing the Problem: When and How? That leaves the question, how best to accomplish the task. The economic imperatives calling for a bold, comprehensive economic program are clear. But knowing that something needs to be done, and having a reasonably clear idea of what the solution is, leaves unanswered the question of tactics. When and how?

The answer to the question "When?" is relatively easy—"Now!" There is never an easy time to do difficult things. There is broad agreement and overwhelming public acknowledgement that the federal budget is largely out of control and that federal budget restraint is economically necessary. But while almost everyone recognizes the general problems, consensus dissipates and resolve weakens when changes in specific programs are considered. While restraining the growth in federal spending is difficult any time, there are several reasons why it will likely be easier now than later. Historically, presidential popularity is highest at the beginning of a term. During the so-called "honeymoon" period the public and the Congress are more inclined to "give the President and his programs a chance." Moreover, the Democrats, having not only decisively lost the White House, but also now a minority in the Senate for the first time in 26 years, are somewhat reluctant initially to challenge the Republican electoral mandate. For the moment, the spending constituencies are not in the ascendance. With no general elections until November 1982 the leverage of organized spending interests is at its nadir.

Over time the honeymoon period will end, organized

interest groups will regain their strength and aggressiveness, and the clock will move inexorably toward another campaign season for the Congress. Politically, the time is now to attempt the most difficult tasks.

Moreover, should the economy remain in its current disarray, the administration could quickly lose control of the economic policy agenda. By summer, ignited by a weak economy, the Congress could press for a host of measures to stimulate the economy generally and to shore up particularly weak sectors such as autos, housing, thrift institutions, and small businesses. Under such circumstances, the administration could easily find itself on the defensive, constantly opposing ill-conceived though well meaning bail-out schemes. We would essentially be reduced to reacting to events and congressional initiatives rather than shaping the economic agenda.

The legislative calendar provides a "once only" opportunity to implement such a strategy in the need for a reconciliation of the FY 1981 budget. The second congressional budget resolution for FY 1981 established a legally binding budget ceiling of $632.4 billion. However, federal outlays during FY 1981 are currently estimated at $661 billion. The need is obvious for a reconciliation of the FY 1981 budget. It must be completed soon.

The important opportunity presented by the reconciliation process is not so much what we can acheive in terms of FY 1981 (although we should be able to achieve a

2 percent reduction in outlays—roughly $13 billion), but permanent changes in entitlement and obligational authority that will mean even larger savings in FY 1982, FY 1983, and FY 1984. Indeed, without such permanent changes, the prospects for getting the budget effectively under control in subsequent years are greatly diminished. By using the reconciliation process, the battle to gain control of the federal budget will concentrate the righting in a limited period when your relative strength is high.

Thus, if the administration's four-year spending control battle is to be won, a plan to permanently reduce the size of the federal budget must be launched within two or three weeks of the inauguration and must be the lead element in the total economic package.

There is another reason why it is important for the administration to propose its budget control package early. Without a credible prior down payment on expenditure reduction, the Reagan tax plan will likely generate intense political controversy during the legislative process. Professional economic opinion and Wall Street sentiment could run against a major tax cut in the absence of real spending restraint. This could lead to substantial revisions in the administration's tax proposals (limiting the plan to one year and substituting business cuts and credits for personal rate reductions) and the unpleasant choice of the President either signing a bill that is not his own or vetoing the measure. The strains on Republican unity could be severe.

Public attitudes also reflect the value of linking and sequencing the budget control and tax reduction portions of the economic program. On the one hand, cutting federal spending (as a single option) is much preferred to cutting taxes. On the other hand, the fear that tax reductions in the absence of significant spending reductions will accelerate the rate of inflation is strong.

In short, there is a need to focus congressional attention on spending reductions along with tax cuts. In addition to the necessary reconciliation process, it would be helpful to have a powerful action-focusing event to hold congressional feet to the fire. The tool is readily available in the national debt ceiling. The present debt ceiling authority is $935 billion. Outstanding national debt will have reached the $930 billion mark by January 20th. This means that one of the President's first requests to the Congress will unavoidably be a debt ceiling increase to prevent the government from defaulting.

The strategic opportunity here is to ask for only a 100-day extension and a dollar increase sufficient to finance the government through that period. This would create a fixed time for action on the spending package. The President would then present his comprehensive economic program, offering it as the only way to prevent the federal government from heading over the one-trillion-dollar national debt level before the end of calendar 1981 sharp budget cuts are made. The symbolism of a trillion-dollar national debt could be used to good effect in forcing attention on the need to reverse the pattern of persistent and growing annual deficits.

Most Americans are terribly uninformed about the size of the national debt, but, contrarily, express considerable concern about a debt at the trillion-dollar level. Fully eighty percent (80%) of those interviewed thought the national debt was below $800 billion with many (59%) under the impression that the total national debt was less than $500 billion. Over one-third thought it under $100 billion. Six out of ten Americans said that a federal debt of a trillion dollars would cause them a great deal of concern. Fifty-seven percent (57%) indicate that even if they agreed with a candidate running for Congress on almost all issues, they would vote against him if he did not think it was important to try to limit the debt to something under one trillion dollars. Without question, the symbolism of a trillion-dollar national debt should be skillfully used in generating citizen and grassroots support for the administration's budget control program.

As it is almost certain that over the next two years the debt will break the trillion-dollar level, it must be made clear to the public that:

- The debt is a legacy left us by the past administration.

PRESIDENT RONALD REAGAN'S

- Even though it is possible, over the next two-year period, that the trillion-dollar debt level will be exceeded, all reasonable and prudent steps must be taken now to get the debt generated by the federal government under control by cutting spending.

- Federal debt fuels inflation. Inflation hurts all Americans and especially our oldest and youngest citizens. (Too frequently Republicans speak of the debt in accounting terms when they should speak about it in human terms.) Or, more generally stated, our ultimate interest is not "programs" or "policies," but how these in turn impact <u>people</u> for the better.

LEADERSHIP AND DEVELOPING
THE ECONOMIC PROGRAM

THE WAY IN which a program is developed can significantly influence its acceptance. It is crucial that the Congress and the country perceive the Reagan expenditure control package as equitable and balanced. Two things will strongly shape their perception. First, the extent to which your proposals for restraining spending fall on all groups and sectors in our society. Second, the process by which you develop your proposals. Are key congressional figures adequately consulted? Do department and agency heads feel ignored or excluded? Do major constituencies feel they had a chance to be heard?

The American people want a presidency that is open but orderly, that conveys the sense of careful, systematic, balanced deliberation, not confusion. This will be difficult in view of the severe time constraints. But it is important. Part of the problem of the Carter programs was the image of haphazard external consultations (relations with the Congress were consistently reported as poor) and internal confusion.

The way in which the economic program is developed and articulated will form important first impressions about the administration and about the President's capacity to lead the federal government. It will help set the pattern for relations with the Congress, with the business and labor communities, and between the White House and cabinet departments and agencies.

It will also communicate a sense of priorities and the level of presidential commitment to his programs. What does he really want and how persistently will he work to get it?

When Jimmy Carter assumed the Presidency he tried to move on many fronts simultaneously—energy, welfare reform, government reorganization, a tax stimulus package, tax reform. It left the Congress and the country unsure about what he really cared about. He had so many priorities that he had no priorities. After a frantic week in announcing his energy program, a struggle he called the "moral equivalent of war," he seemingly lost interest in the issue. He laid it all out and expected the country and the Congress to respond. He failed to realize that leadership means more than "laying it all out"; it also means keeping at it.

The serious economic problems we face present a great challenge but also a great opportunity. The American people yearn for a leader with a sense of vision, who knows what is needed, and is willing to lead the country, whatever the price, down that path.

FOREIGN POLICY AT THE BEGINNING

NOTHING DESTABILIZES THE international system more than a superpower that has lost its way in the world. Hence, nothing would contribute more to international stability and to domestic revitalization in the United States, including economic recovery, than the United States recovering its confidence, leadership, and margin of safety in world affairs.

Unfortunately the prevailing sense among many Americans, and the country's allies and adversaries, is that the United States is uncertain of its national interests and role in world affairs. United States foreign policy has recently been fraught with ambiguity, uncertainty, and inconsistency. Worse still is the growing view that America has grown weak in its foreign policy resolve, in its defense posture, and in its ability to respond to security threats around the globe.

The principal policy objectives of the foreign and defense

policy of the new administration in the initial phase are to establish the President's credibility and leadership in foreign affairs, and the country's commitment to peace through developing a new margin of safety. This objective will signal the American people and the rest of the world that President Reagan is committed to giving direction and consistency to America's foreign policy, thereby enabling the country to play a constructive role in world affairs. It is imperative that the President's actions in the first ninety days include visible resource commitments and other concrete actions to support his statements and that these commitments be made in a strategic context that suggests sustained resolve beyond the first ninety days of the new administration.

The return of the hostages now provides an ideal opportunity for the President to define a new U.S. policy toward international terrorism that will both reduce the probability of another Iranian Embassy take-over and will signal the direction and a new consistency in our foreign policy.

A new margin of safety will be achieved by our willingness to commit sufficient resources to rearm American foreign policy in defense, intelligence, information, and foreign assistance areas. Clear signals must be sent out early that while the Reagan Administration recognizes military power is not a policy panacea, it also recognizes that it is vital; and the United States does not intend to confront the international challenges of the 1980's poorly armed or hesitant to use military force when appropriate. Supplemental budget increases are essential to augment the fighting readiness of defense units to reduce vulnerabilities in our deterrent forces, and to improve the collection and analysis activities, as well as morale, of our intelligence community. The effect will be to increase the confidence of our friends and the deterrence of our adversaries.

These budget increases are manageable if prepared with care, proper targeting, and exacting cost-efficiency. They contrast with the sobering cuts in spending on the domestic side and therefore must be managed with care. But this contrast increases their significance as a signal to the domestic public, allies and adversaries alike. Domestic budget requirements cannot be an excuse for insufficient defense and foreign policy commitments. After all, that is precisely the excuse our allies use. Where, then, is the demonstration of new American leadership?

Presenting a budget that cuts spending in many entitlement programs while increasing spending in defense areas is the approach public opinion currently supports. It is essential to seize this opportunity early. The impact on the psychology of the American people in the two most important areas of current malaise—foreign policy and economic conditions—will be dramatic. And in one area in particular—energy, the perception of a stronger American defense commitment in the Middle East may go a long way to reassure oil producers (e.g., Kuwait, Saudi Arabia, etc.) in this area to sustain and perhaps even increase oil production, preventing another major world and domestic oil price increase arising from the Iran-Iraq war.

STRATEGIC OBJECTIVES

THE ADMINISTRATION CAN meet the requirement to re-establish confidence, leadership, and muscle in U.S. foreign policy and defense programs through the following long-range strategic objectives:

- Restore the margin of safety in U.S. security by laying out a long-range, multi-year defense program.

- Strengthen U.S. foreign policy by revitalizing intelligence, information, and foreign assistance programs.

- Respond to fundamental problems of Soviet power, allied and third world diversity, and interdependence, managing crises (hostages, Poland, Central America, etc.) in a context of confidence and conviction about where we are heading.

- Establish a strong collaborative relationship with U.S. allies as the springboard for conducting foreign relations during the term.

- Establish a significant presence in the Middle East to deter Soviet intervention, local instability, and the cutoff of vital oil supplies to the West.

It is never easy to establish a new policy footing, but it will never be more appropriate or more possible than in the early days of the administration. The President has an opportunity that will not persist indefinitely. It is essential that the message to the public, America's allies, and its adversaries communicates an unequivocal commitment to upgrading the fighting readiness of U.S. forces and supporting U.S. foreign policy initiatives by a refurbished intelligence, information, and foreign assistance posture.

The essential political goal desired in the initial period is to change the image of America as a weak or declining superpower by clarifying the sense of national purpose and taking early policy initiatives that register the country's commitment to a new margin of safety.

EARLY INITIATIVES

SELECTED INITIATIVES SHOULD be given priority in the first ninety days to meet the strategic objectives of restoring U.S. confidence, leadership, and margin of safety. These actions include:

- Submit a FY 1981 defense budget supplemental containing additional outlays for deterrent force, Indian Ocean deployments, and defense preparedness programs.

- Rebuild America's intelligence programs including budget increases for analytical activities in the CIA, State and Defense, for human intelligence, and R&D in technical collection capability.

- Dramatically strengthen information programs (e.g., in ICA, VOA, RFE, BIB) to upgrade the role of these information agencies as instruments of U.S. foreign policy.

- Strengthen and reprogram the foreign assistance programs to obtain maximum flexibility in working with American allies, especially those in unstable regions (e.g. Yemen, Tunisia, Pakistan, etc.)

- Establish an interagency task force to formulate and implement a coordinated U.S. strategy toward the Middle East, including a strategy for negotiating a Sinai security force as called for by the Egyptian-Israeli peace treaty.

- Follow a strategy of foreign visits to Washington which allows the President to stay at home and to focus on receiving heads-of-state, foreign ministers, and ambassadors. The sequencing of these visits should be integrated into the White House communication plan to emphasize important consultations with the allies in the initial period.

INTERNATIONAL CRISES

FAR TOO FREQUENTLY new administrations barely have enough time to assume office before they must respond to an international crisis somewhere in the world. The Reagan Administration will assume office with the hostage situation still dominating the nightly news, the unrest in Poland, the fighting in Afghanistan and between the Iraqis and Iranians, and the instability in Central America.

The Reagan Administration should develop a style of handling crises within a framework of dealing with the more fundamental problems facing the United States, such as Soviet power, growing allied and third world diversity, and increasing economic and social interdependence. Crises should be managed with minimum public drama and maximum private resolve and commitment. To accomplish this, the President, while being seen to be in charge of crises management, should not be involved in minute-by-minute negotiations, thus being manipulated by foreign adversaries.

The past President used crises to refurbish his public image of poor leadership; the new President already has an image of strength and resolve, and indeed was elected, in part, because of that image. The President should be involved in setting the overall approach to crises and in making the key decision during them, but never allowing them to drive or dominate the Presidency. Jimmy Carter allowed himself to become the president of the hostages, rather than the president of the people. In effect his Presidency became the hostage of the crises which resulted in the immobilization and constriction of the President's full range of decision latitude. The country was not well served by this situation.

DOMESTIC POLICY: THE ECONOMIC IMPACT EVALUATION PHASE

THE ECONOMIC PACKAGE must be the centerpiece of the Reagan Administration's early policy initiatives. It is important that the White House not deflect congressional or national attention from the economic program by simultaneously pressing for other major domestic initiatives. The spending control proposals in the economic package will directly affect many domestic programs.

The strategic domestic policy objective for the initial phase should be to evaluate the impact on large domestic programs of the spending control measures that are enacted, and the overall domestic approach and programmatic adjustments the President should take.

An accompanying objective is to use this period to show that while the primary objective is to reduce the size of government to a level where it is more manageable and affordable, <u>it is also the time to think about</u>

domestic programs scaled to human proportions, the social-economic well-being of the people, and the President's approach to governance.

Since the economic package will set the time when domestic policy can emerge from a deliberative policy review (likely well beyond the first ninety-day period), the initial phase should be used to take Presidential action of a compassionate and caring nature, and stimulate an increased sense of volunteerism in America.

The President can use this early opportunity to suggest, for example, more voluntary participation at the community, state, and national levels by all Americans. The values the President-elect described in his Detroit acceptance speech should now begin to be re-articulated as operational components of a new sense of civic duty for Americans. The idea is for the President to make a direct appeal to the American people to encourage them to increase their individual participation in community affairs. It must be remembered that Mr. Reagan is one of the best communicators in America; he is certainly the most important public leader and political communicator. It is essential in this leadership role that during the first ninety days for the President to report that his instincts about government being overextended were correct and that since the election his respect for the capabilities, dedication, and resources of the people has increased even beyond what it was before November 4th.

The President's message should be that the government should do less, and the people should do more. This is especially true in the resolution of many domestic problems in this country.

An excellent opportunity exists for the President to initiate a call for increased volunteerism in America. The President should first seek to motivate citizens to increase their community-level participation, to create a relationship between their local leaders and themselves where the former are viewed as "accountable stewards" and the latter are active participants in local programs seeking to upgrade the quality of life in America. And one action the President might consider is the creation of a "Medics for Peace," where volunteers from the medical profession would freely contribute their time, services, and resources in a time of crisis anywhere in the world upon request. The only government resources needed would be to coordinate such an effort and provide transportation.

The President should also use this initial period to advance the "enterprise zone" idea which he spoke of frequently in the campaign as an attractive alternative approach to urban renewal. The ideal is consistent with President Reagan's public philosophy because it encourages economic growth in the inner cities without government intervention, or public funds. The enterprise zone strategy will allow the President to describe the themes for domestic policy that his administration will support—namely:

- Create an attractive atmosphere for business generally, rather than subsidies for special businesses;

- Focus government energies on difficult social problems to be resolved by innovative strategies in the private sector;

- Limit the government regulations and red tape; and,

- Combat defeatism about the prospects of showing America's complex and pressing domestic challenges.

THE FEDERAL GOVERNMENT'S role in a renewed economic growth strategy for the inner cities should not be to increase Action grants, make available more development loans, or public works projects, but to adopt strategies that contribute to the process whereby the inner cities become self-sustaining, economic entities rather than tax burdens.

SECTION IV

HISTORICAL PERSPECTIVE

History clearly shows how important the first days of any administration are. In every administration since Roosevelt when there has been a regular transfer of power through the election process, the pattern of presidential behavior is established in those first few days when the administration is seeking to exert its control over the government.

The initial actions of the presidency are important because of three principles:

- The first few days of any administration create lasting impressions about the man in the Oval Office.

- The central thrust of the presidency will be defined during the early period.

- As the administration seeks to establish control of the government, it is extremely vulnerable to making big mistakes.

The fact that early impressions are lasting impressions is no surprise to anyone, but in being self-evident we cannot afford to overlook or underestimate the principle's importance. The principal impression desired about the new man in the Oval Office is that a steady, resolute hand is now controlling the ship of state, and that he is presiding over a more orderly governmental process than has been the case in the past.

The central thrust of the new administration will communicate to America what the President thinks is salient and pressing. It will define where the focus of presidential activity will be, and hence the national issue agenda the President intends to pursue. The public will test the content of the President's agenda against their own sense of national priorities. The degree of early congruence will lengthen the President's opportunity to change public policy in this country.

It is impossible to think about the beginning of new administrations without being deeply concerned about the dangers involved in assuming office. Crises, domestic and foreign, are not respectors of new presidents. The decision time, issue complexity, and novelty of many issues can increase dramatically the possibility of an error—in judgment and policy selection. Tensions currently in the world are real and foreboding, and the new administration should trust the record of history which cautions every new President to guard against the foolish big error, e.g., Kennedy's Bay of Pigs, or Carter's energy fiasco, that may be unwittingly made in the first few weeks.

There are commonalities across the first hundred days of the different administrations that are worth noting.

Presidential Travel

- With the exception of Nixon's trip to Europe, presidents have <u>not</u> made trips overseas.

- In lieu of foreign travel by the President, it has been customary for the Vice President or the Secretary of State to undertake an early foreign visit.

- Also the amount of domestic travel of the President is somewhat limited during the initial period.

Speeches, Press Conferences, and Statements

- State of the Union addresses were given by two presidents—Eisenhower and Kennedy—while Roosevelt called an extraordinary session of Congress the day after inauguration. Nixon and Carter did not give State of the Union addresses.

- Eisenhower gave ten radio speeches to the country and set the most active pace in this regard even though two of Roosevelt's famous fireside chats were given within the first one hundred days. Kennedy and Nixon did not give addresses in this fashion. Carter's twist was to give two television addresses and one call-in radio program where he answered questions.

- The general pattern is for presidents to address selected groups on an average of once every two weeks.

- The trend associated with press conferences was to hold them every two to three weeks with the first one coming in the second week or so of the new administration. (President Roosevelt was a marked exception to the pattern because he averaged one press conference every five days.)

Important Symbolic Gestures

- Presidents have frequently used the first hundred days to make a symbolic outreach gesture that they wanted incorporated in the central theme and image of the new administration. This was particularly true of John F. Kennedy, whose gestures included: Food for Peace, the Alliance for Progress, Frost's role in the inauguration, and the Youth Fitness Council. These are style, tone, and policy setting gestures which differentiate the focus of the new presidency from its predecessors.

• Other examples include Roosevelt's Good Neighbor Policy, Nixon's European and 14th Street corridor visits, and Carter's letter to Soviet dissidents and financial disclosures for Cabinet officers.

Meetings

• Cabinet meetings vary depending on the degree of reliance on them to govern. The pattern has been to hold them about once a week. The two exceptions have been Roosevelt, who held them twice a week, and Kennedy, who held only one of them in the first hundred days.

• Meetings with Congressional leaders have generally averaged once a week. Kennedy and FDR did, however, hold these consultations more frequently.

- There has been at least one event with the President's own political party.

- Presidents have taken the opportunity to visit the departments; Nixon visited thirteen of them and Carter went to eight.

Vacations

- None of the presidents surveyed have taken vacations in the first hundred days.

The first-ever release of the document that guided Reagan to unprecedented success in his first six months in office and the years that followed.

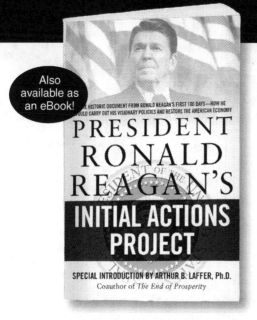

Also available as an eBook!

THE HISTORIC DOCUMENT FROM RONALD REAGAN'S FIRST 100 DAYS—HOW HE WOULD CARRY OUT HIS VISIONARY POLICIES AND RESTORE THE AMERICAN ECONOMY

PRESIDENT RONALD REAGAN'S

INITIAL ACTIONS PROJECT

SPECIAL INTRODUCTION BY ARTHUR B. LAFFER, Ph.D.
Coauthor of *The End of Prosperity*

President Ronald Reagan's Initial Actions Project is a blueprint of how Reagan's economic policies were achieved.

As a model for a new president facing the daunting demands of a nation in turmoil, the significance of the IAP report has never been more timely. History proves that President Reagan's policies led to economic growth; will Barack Obama overturn this invaluable legacy? Only time—and history—will tell.

Available at www.simonandschuster.com

THRESHOLD
EDITIONS
A Division of Simon & Schuster
A CBS COMPANY

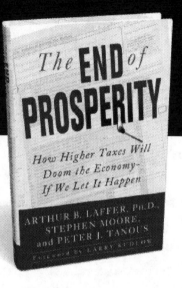

Printed in the United States
By Bookmasters